Oceans
and Marine Life

By
Stéphanie Babin

Illustrated by
Lucile Ahrweiller
Hélène Convert
Deborah Pinto
Emmanuel Ristord

Twirl

Contents

A Day by the Ocean   24

Port   26

Fish Market   28

Aquaculture   30

Looking for Small Creatures   32

Lighthouses   34

Water Sports   36

Scuba Diving   38

Let's Review!   40

Oceans, Seas, and More!   6

The Blue Planet   8

The Ocean Floor   10

Warm Waters   12

Cold Waters   14

Along the Coastline   16

Tides   18

Storms   20

Let's Review!   22

A Day at the Beach   42

What to Bring   44

The Beach   46

Beach Games   48

Swimming   50

Picnic   52

Let's Review!   54

Ocean Vehicles 56

Boats 58

Sailboat 60

Ocean Liner 62

Submarine 64

Let's Review! 66

More to Know

Oceans and Seas 82

The Water Cycle 84

The Food Chain 86

Damaging the Ocean 88

Preserving the Ocean 90

Index 92

Marine Animals 68

Fish 70

Mammals 71

Tropical Ocean Wildlife ... 72

Temperate Ocean Wildlife ... 74

Ocean Giants 76

Aquarium 78

Let's Review! 80

? The "Let's Review!" pages at the end of each section help reinforce learning.

The "More to Know" section at the end of the book provides additional information to help you understand the subject.

Index Quickly find the word you're looking for with the index at the end of the book.

Look for the colored boxes in the bottom right-hand corners. You will find references to related subjects in other parts of the book.

Oceans, Seas,
and More!

The Blue Planet

Water is essential for life, and there's a lot of it on our planet. Bodies of water come in all shapes and sizes, including large oceans and seas, long rivers, small bays, swamps, and even ice sheets.

ice sheet

river

sea

ocean

You can visit an ice sheet,

a riverbank,

a rocky coast of a sea,

or an ocean shore.

How
are seas and oceans different ?

When you look out at a sea, you can't see the other side. Way over there is the horizon. The sea continues far beyond it.

But there's something even bigger: an ocean! Oceans are enormous, have bigger waves, and are deeper than seas.

To cross an ocean in an airplane, you may have to spend a whole school day flying!

Oceans and Seas **82**
The Water Cycle **84**

The Ocean Floor

Mountains, volcanoes, deep trenches . . .
The bottom of the ocean is not flat!

beach

buoy

moray eel

sperm whale

shipwreck

underwater volcano

abyssal plain

10

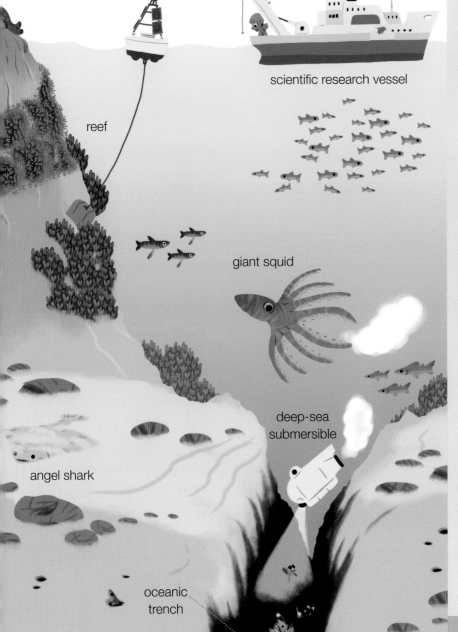

What

might you find deep underwater ?

scientific research vessel

reef

giant squid

deep-sea submersible

angel shark

oceanic trench

At the beach, when the water is clear, you can see the bottom. But as you go farther out, the water gets darker.

In the ocean, there are places so deep that no one has ever explored them. Even submarines and submersibles can't go there!

Deep underwater, there's no light, and there are fish we haven't discovered yet. What do you think they look like?

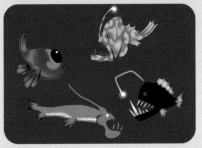

11

🌴 Warm Waters

Around the equator, the temperatures of the air and the sea are warmer than they are in other parts of the world.

volcano

inlet to the lagoon

outrigger canoe

blacktip reef shark

sea turtle

swimmer

fishing net

snorkeler

parrotfish

fishing village

pelican

seashells

umbrella

sand

What
is coral

?

ocean liner

palm tree

coral reef

cottages

banana tree

Uh-oh! Someone's getting a sunburn.

hotel

You can find corals in the sand on certain beaches. Do you think it is a plant, a shell, a pebble, or a seaweed?

A coral is actually made up of tiny animals that live clumped together underwater. They feed on plankton by using their tentacles.

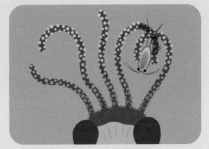

Corals are helpful ocean creatures, but fishing and pollution harm them. You can see corals when you scuba dive, snorkel, or visit an aquarium.

Tropical Ocean Wildlife **72**
Oceans and Seas **82**

Cold Waters

The Arctic is Earth's northernmost region. That's where you'll find the coldest ocean, the Arctic Ocean.

auks

rocky cliff

research station

arctic fox

tracked vehicle

seal

reindeer

musk ox

sea ice

snowmobile

husky

snow petrel

iceberg

walrus

orca

polar bear

ice sheet

icebreaker

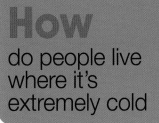

How

do people live where it's extremely cold ?

In many parts of the world, it gets cold in the winter. At the North and South Poles, it can be *very* cold most of the time!

How do animals cope? The animals' bodies have adapted, and they have thick fur or feathers. Some animals go elsewhere during the winter.

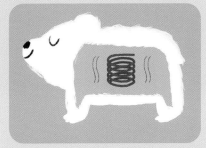

You can get used to different climates, too. In the summer, you might wear a T-shirt and light clothing. What might you wear in the winter?

Along the Coastline

On the coasts, the sea is warm enough to swim in, but only in the summer.

pine tree

cliff

lighthouse

rock

ocean

waves

reef

sailboat

gannet

coastal footpath

heather

gorse

green flag

pebbles

lifeguard station

sea-foam

swimming area

seaweed

sand

seawall

seagull

31 05 75G

fishing trawler

If you look at waves, you'll see that they rise and fall. Their movement depends on how hard the wind blows.

Over time, the waves wear away rocks by crashing into them. Gradually, the coastal landscape changes.

The waves also toss pebbles, sand, shells, and other things onto the shore. What have you found on a beach?

Looking for Small Creatures **32**

The Beach **46**

17

 Tides

The water level of the oceans rises and falls throughout the day.

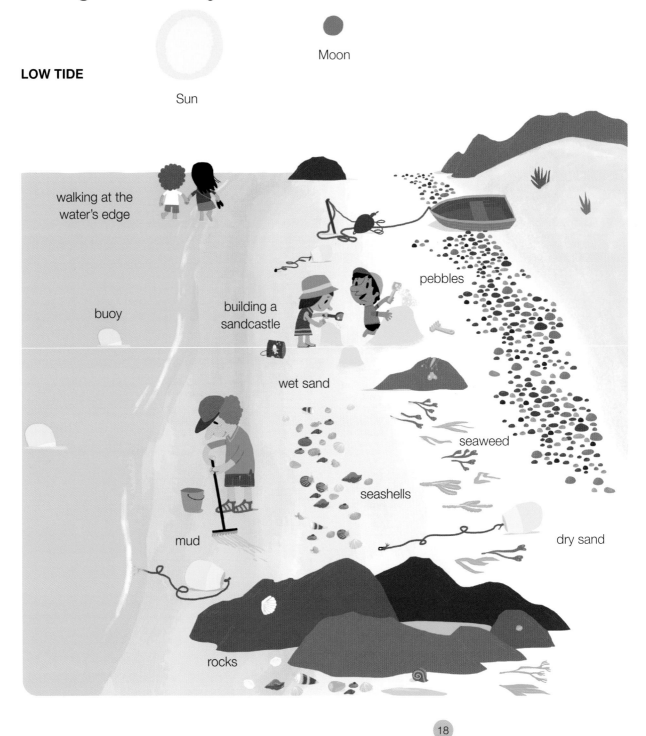

Moon

Sun

LOW TIDE

walking at the water's edge

buoy

building a sandcastle

pebbles

wet sand

seaweed

seashells

mud

dry sand

rocks

Sun

HIGH TIDE

launching
a boat

mooring
buoy

wave

jumping in
the wave

Where
do tides come from
?

When water approaches the shore little by little, that's a rising tide. When it moves away, that's an ebbing tide.

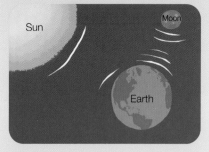

Tides are caused mainly by the Moon's gravity pulling the ocean toward it. Gravity from Earth and the Sun also affects the tides, but not as much as the Moon.

Sun

Moon

Earth

The more water there is, the greater the difference between tides. Do you think tides are more visible in a sea or in an ocean?

Atlantic
Ocean

Mediterranean
Sea

Looking for Small Creatures **32**
Oceans and Seas **82**

Storms

When the wind blows hard
and the clouds are gray,
the waters rise.

thunderstorm

lightning

lighthouse

swell

signal flare

boat
accident

waves

reef

oilskin raincoat
and hat

lifeboat

buoy

tugboat

breakwater

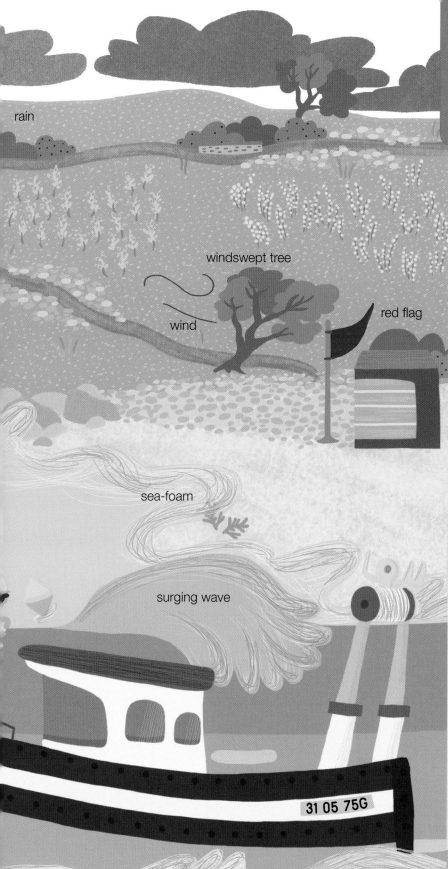

rain

windswept tree

wind

red flag

sea-foam

surging wave

31 05 75G

Why
are there
colored flags **?**

You feel like going for a swim, but you're out of luck. An adult points to the red flag and says, "No, not today!"

To know whether you can go in the water, look at the flags. Green: safe to swim; orange: be careful; red: off-limits!

Sometimes, even without waves, there are currents in the water. Swimmers can get caught in them, which is dangerous.

21

Along the Coastline **16**
Swimming **50**

Can you name these animals? Which ones can you find in places where the ocean water is cold?

What do you think the weather is like in this picture? Is the ocean calm or rough?
Who is in danger?

Where are these three children standing?

Where might you find these fish?

Look closely at what these people are wearing. Where do each of them live?

Our planet is enormous.
Do you know where you live?
Do you live on a coast? Or near a river?

A Day by the Ocean

 # Port

This is where fishing trawlers line up
and unload their catch.

jetty

warehouse

dock

moving the catch

crane

unloading
the catch

fishing trawler

fish tubs

ice

21 22 23 24

fishing trawler

entrance to harbor

breakwater

Nicolas Bouvier

nets

tying up
a boat

4211

2320

mooring
bollard

quay

shellfish tubs

How
do you catch
a lot of fish
?

Line fishing is very slow. You have to wait a long time for a fish to take the bait on your hook.

Fishing trawlers, on the other hand, use huge nets. The boats throw them into the water, then pull up a lot of fish!

Unfortunately, people may be fishing more than they need to. Overfishing can leave the oceans without fish, and that could have a huge effect on marine life.

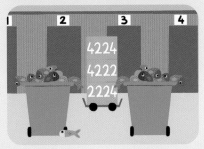

1   2   3   4

4224
4222
2224

Fish Market

At the port, vendors sell the fish that the fishermen have just caught.

seagull

fishmonger

weighing the fish

$6/lb

periwinkle snails

mussels

$14/lb

$14/lb

$13/lb

$12/lb

salmon

sea urchins

$11/lb

red mullets

tuna

ice

sea bream

$10/lb $10/lb

bass

squid

fishmonger's stall

Why
do we eat fish

?

goustine

$8 /lb

$6 /lb

shrimp

fishmonger

$8

fish pâté

$20 /lb

$11 /lb

$4

$10 /lb

crab

fish soup

$12

lobsters

spider crab

bisque

shellfish and
fish products

Fish is good for your health.

It contains many vitamins and
minerals that your body needs
to be strong and healthy.

Besides fish, there are other sea
creatures you can eat, including
crabs and mussels. Have you
ever eaten shrimp?

Aquaculture **30**
Looking for Small Creatures **32**

 # Aquaculture

Aquaculture is the farming of fish and shellfish, shells, and even salt from the sea.

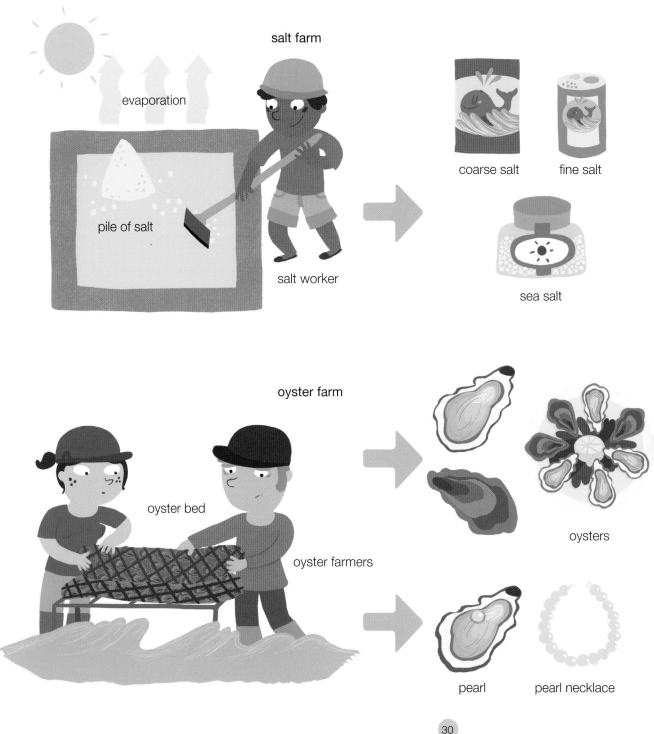

salt farm

evaporation

pile of salt

salt worker

coarse salt   fine salt

sea salt

oyster farm

oyster bed

oyster farmers

oysters

pearl   pearl necklace

30

mussel farm

mussels

open mussel

plate of mussels
and fries

shrimp farm

shrimp

peeled shrimp

sushi rolls wrapped
in seaweed

seaweed farm

seaweed

ingredient in food

How

does fish get to your plate?

If you live far from the ocean, fish and shellfish sometimes take a long trip to get to you.

A refrigerated truck picks up the fish at the port and travels all the way to a store near you.

Your parents buy the fish in a store. Sometimes it was packaged beforehand in a factory. Do you like fish sticks?

Looking for Small Creatures

At low tide, all you need are some tools and patience to find these little animals.

sea star

sea urchin

weever

clar

clamming fork

cockleshell

rake

raking
the sand

smooth
clams

razor clam

otter shell

winkle

mussels

warty venu

abalone

whelk

What
is a shell

jellyfish

wet sand

crab

rocks

sea anemone

hermit crab

limpet

shrimp

dip net

blenny

Shells that have washed up on the beach are almost always empty.

The shells were once the homes of various sea creatures, including mussels, clams, and hermit crabs.

In the sand, underneath the pebbles, you can find living shellfish. Do you know which ones are edible?

🗼 Lighthouses

These tall towers along coastlines shine a very bright light that can be seen from far away.

light bulb

lens

guardrail

tower

spiral staircase

pedestal

wharf

sea shuttle

120390C

the coast

During the day

beam of light

At night

Maybe you've visited a lighthouse while on vacation. At the top is a light that's like a huge lamp.

At night the light is visible to boats from a distance. It lets the sailors know that a port is nearby or that there are rocks.

Today, to help sailors find their way, many boats use computers that are similar to the GPS you might use in the car.

🛟 Water Sports

These are all sports activities you can do on the water for fun.

parasailing

pedal boat

Jet Ski

speedboat

water-skiing

kitesurfing

kayak

snorkeling

bodyboarding

What

type of boat should you try first ?

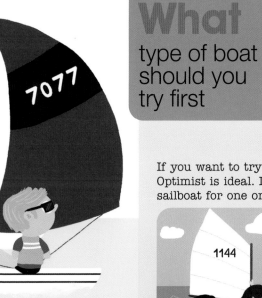

7077

7077

catamaran

competing in a boat race

4214

Optimist sailing dinghies

4411

sailing instructor

surfing

windsurfing

If you want to try boating, the Optimist is ideal. It's a small sailboat for one or two people.

1144

A sailing instructor teaches you to steer the boat. Push the tiller to the right to make the boat turn left!

4211

A pedal boat is a fun way to enjoy the water. All you need is foot power!

Boats 58
Sailboat 60

Scuba Diving

This is an amazing sport for discovering the wonders of the ocean floor.

dive flag

diver

boat

grouper

seahorse

shipwreck

parrotfish

coral

treasure

moray eel

diving hood

diving mask

glove

wet suit

weight belt

dive light

diving boot

dive fin

...uba regulator ...r breathing

depth gauge for measuring how deep you are

cylinder of compressed air

How

do you breathe underwater

?

When you put your head underwater, you hold your breath. It's natural! Your body knows not to breathe in water.

When you go scuba diving, you breathe "bottled" air from a cylinder. There's enough air in each tank to breathe for about one hour.

Have you ever seen bubbles around divers when they are underwater? That's the air that divers breathe out.

Warm Waters **12**
Water Sports **36**

Let's Review!

Is this boat returning to or leaving the harbor? What is this type of boat called?

Which of these small animals can you find in the sand?
Do you know what they're called?

Look carefully at these pictures. Which one shows a person who is sailing?

4214

What is this diver missing in order
to breathe underwater?

What small creatures are these children trying to catch?

fisherman

salt worker

sailing instructor

Many jobs are connected to the ocean.
Would you like to work near the sea?
Which job would you like to have when you grow up?

diving instructor

fishmonger

A Day at
the Beach

What to Bring

When you go to the beach, there are important things you shouldn't forget!

snacks

bottle of water

beach mat

cap

sunglasses

arm floaties

T-shirt

swim trunks

sandals

change of clothes

beach umbrella

beach chair

sunscreen spray

sun hat

sunglasses

swimsuit

beach bag

cover-up

sunscreen

flip-flops

magazine

beach towel

You want to do just one thing: go swimming! But before you can, your parents put a hat and sunscreen on you.

In the summer, the Sun is very strong. You have to protect your head, skin, and eyes. Otherwise you'll get sunburn, and that hurts!

After a while, the sunscreen wears off. Don't forget to ask the grown-ups to give you more.

The Beach **46**
Beach Games **48**

The Beach

Fresh air, room to play,
sand, and beautiful waves.
Hooray for the beach!

parking

sand dune

lifeguard

shower

beach
umbrella

tent

cabins

food cart

putting on
sunscreen

SNACKS

restrooms

playground

trampoline

swing

campers

beach camp

sand yacht

Why
do you have to stay in the shade sometimes ?

Even if you've put on sunscreen, sometimes your parents will ask you to stay under the beach umbrella or stop running around.

The Sun can sometimes make you sick: That's called sunstroke. You might get a headache or a fever, and you might throw up.

To avoid getting sick, you have to rest in the shade from time to time. But there are lots of other things you can still do: play cards, build a sandcastle, or read!

 # Beach Games

The beach is an awesome playground where kids and grown-ups can enjoy all kinds of activities.

burying Dad in the sand

building a sandcastle

bucket

sieve

mold

rake

shovel

watering can

bocce ball

balls

Frisbee

ball

racket

marble race

collecting
seashells

catching
shrimp

climbing on
the rocks

playing
pretend

What
is sand

?

It sticks to your feet, gets into everything, and is perfect for making castles. Did you know the sand is not the same at every beach?

different types of beach sand

Sand is made up of tiny, broken, worn pieces of rock, pebbles, dust, shells, coral debris, and other items.

Sand can be used to help make many things, like glass or buildings. Where can you find sand other than at the beach?

Swimming

There's nothing more fun than jumping and playing in the water!

toy boat

green flag
(means it's safe
to swim)

lifeguard

stung by
a weever

THE BEACH
IS OPEN!

Air temp:
81°F (27°C)

Water temp:
77°F (25°C)

beach ball

sea-foam

getting
a mouthful
of seawater

swim ring

arm floaties

floating on
her back

inflatable raft

What
if you're afraid of the water

?

jumping in the wave

buoy

doing the crawl stroke

playing catch

doing the backstroke

ripples

doing the breaststroke

snorkeling

Do the waves scare you a little? Does the ocean seem too big? Many people are afraid to go swimming.

You can take it slow: Dip just your toes in, or get carried by a parent. Little by little, you will get used to being in the water.

Which would you use for your first steps into the water: a swim ring, arm floaties, or an inflatable vest?

 # Picnic

A picnic means eating outdoors. It's a great way to enjoy a day at the beach!

beach umbrella

seagull

picnic basket

drinking from a canteen

relaxing

plastic utensils

salad

hard-boiled eggs

container

pizza

cake

tomatoes

melon

napkin

eating ice cream

sandwich

fries

flask

rock

picking up food scraps

picnic blanket

52

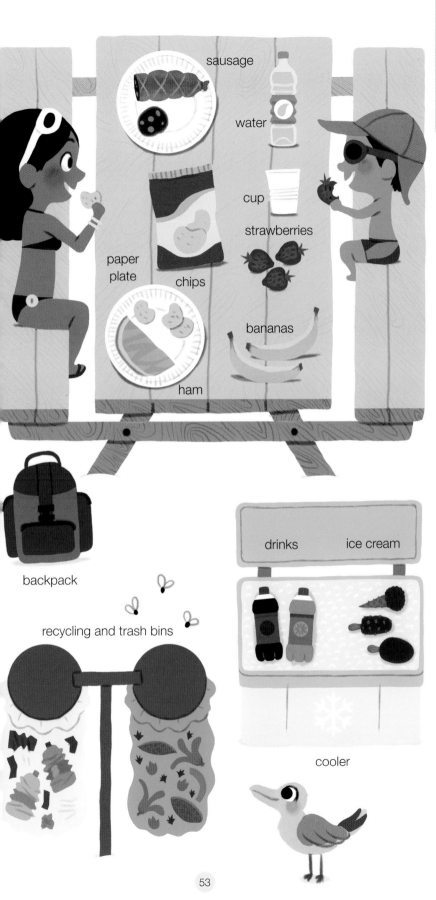

sausage

water

cup

strawberries

bananas

paper plate

chips

ham

backpack

recycling and trash bins

drinks   ice cream

cooler

What
do you eat at a picnic

?

In the summer, the Sun's rays are very strong. Your body sweats and you feel hot. Be sure to drink lots of water. Cold foods, like ice cream, will cool you down too.

Fruits and vegetables are good picnic foods because you don't have to cook them and they are so refreshing.

Don't forget: After a picnic, you have to pick up everything and leave nothing on the sand. If you did not, what would happen?

Damaging the Ocean **88**
Preserving the Ocean **90**

Let's Review!

What do you think are important things to remember to bring to the beach?

Which foods are eaten cold? Which ones are eaten hot?

Which can you use to protect yourself from the Sun?

Who forgot to put on sunscreen? How do you know?

Can you connect each picture to the correct flag?

As you grow up, you will probably learn to swim.
Do you already know how to swim?
Do you use arm floaties or a swim ring?
Do you know different ways to swim?

Ocean
Vehicles

 # Boats

Getting around on the water, traveling, or transporting goods—there's a different boat for each activity!

racing trimaran

sailboat

Optimist sailing dinghy

motorboat

speedboat

fishing trawler

rigid inflatable boat

yacht

ocean liner

ferry

coast guard boat

tall ship

junk

airboat

outrigger canoe

cargo ship

aircraft carrier

How
do boats move

?

In the bathtub, your toy boats move because you push them. On the ocean, it's different. Sailboats move with the help of their sails and the wind.

Other boats are powered by a motor, which turns an underwater propeller that pushes the boat forward.

A rowboat is powered by your arms! You pull the paddle through the water, from front to back. What happens if you pull from back to front?

Water Sports **36**
Sailboat **60**

Sailboat

This is a boat that is powered
by the wind blowing on its sails.

mast

mainsail

lighthouse

skipper

coast

boom

life buoy

tiller

cabin

fender

rudder

hull

keel

flag

jib

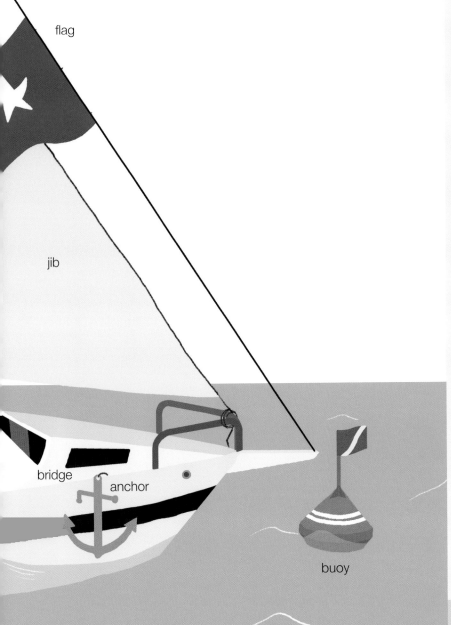

bridge

anchor

buoy

What
do you need to know to drive a boat

?

It might seem easy to steer a sailboat, but there are a lot of things to know because the ocean can be dangerous.

Driving a boat with a motor is like driving a car: You need to take lessons before getting a license.

Recognizing flags, tying knots, studying the winds—it's never too early to learn what you can about being on the water.

Water Sports **36**
Boats **58**

Ocean Liner

This is a huge ship that takes long voyages across oceans.

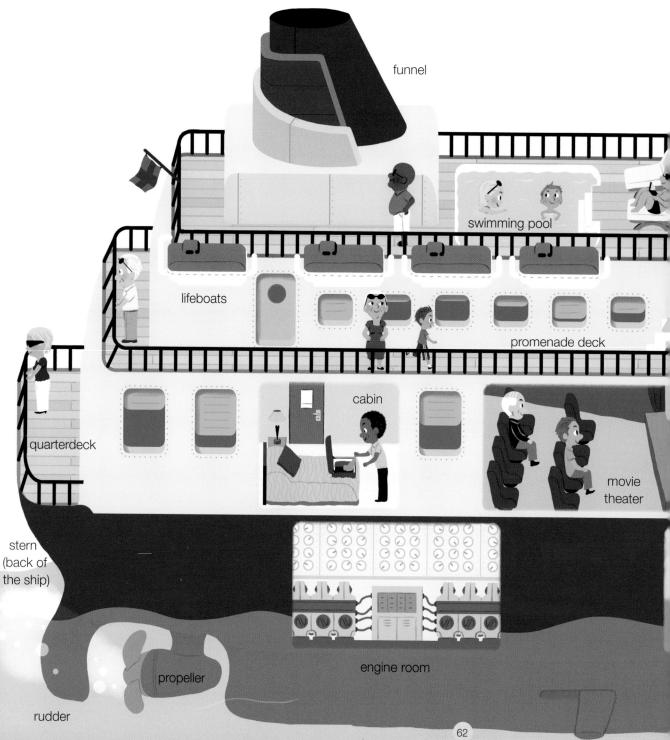

funnel

swimming pool

lifeboats

promenade deck

cabin

quarterdeck

movie theater

stern (back of the ship)

engine room

propeller

rudder

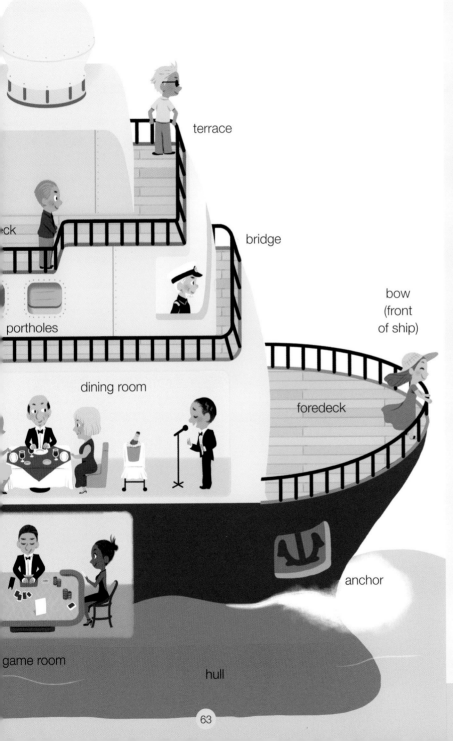

dome that protects
radar system

terrace

ck

bridge

portholes

bow
(front
of ship)

dining room

foredeck

anchor

game room

hull

Why
does an ocean
liner float
?

With its metal hull and engines,
an ocean liner is very heavy.
It should sink, and yet it travels
all the way across the ocean!

It floats because it's full of
air on the inside. Air is much
lighter than water, so the ocean
liner stays afloat.

Try floating a drinking glass in
your bathtub. It doesn't sink,
because it's full of air. The same
is true of boats!

Submarine

This is a ship that can travel
deep underwater.

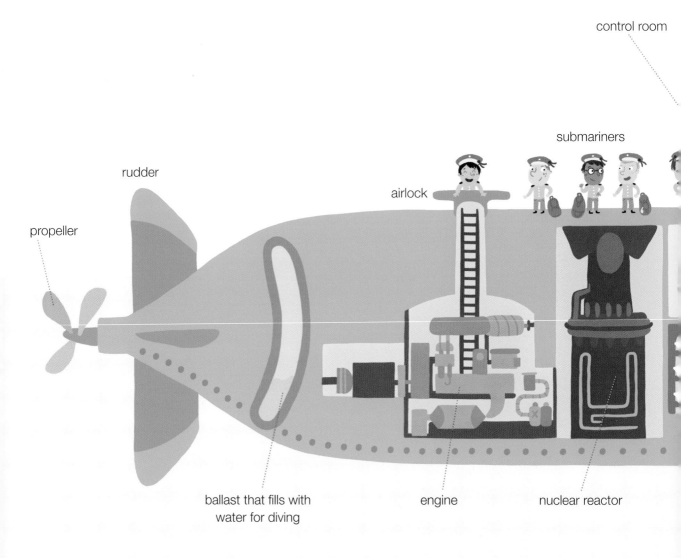

control room

submariners

rudder

airlock

propeller

ballast that fills with
water for diving

engine

nuclear reactor

radar
system

periscope

cabin

mess deck

torpedoes

ballast that fills with
water for diving

sonar

Submarines don't have portholes. Deep in the ocean, the water is also completely dark. So how do you find your way?

If you can't see anything, you have to listen! With a device called sonar, the submariners can hear the sounds around the submarine.

These sounds warn them about objects in their path and signal the presence of another submarine or boat nearby.

Let's Review!

Which of these boats would you use to cross an entire ocean?

 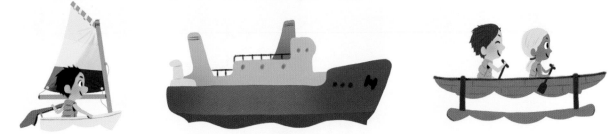

Which of these boats do you think is the fastest?

Which of these boats does not need the wind to move?

Cabins are where you sleep on a boat. Which of these is found on an ocean liner, and which is found on a submarine?

 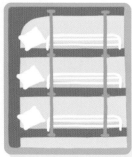

What is this sailboat missing so it can move?

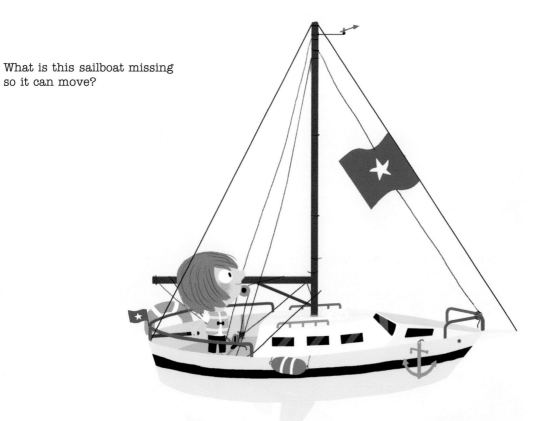

There are many ocean vehicles, including pedal boats, rowboats, and sailboats. Which ones have you ridden in? If you haven't been in any, which would you like to try? Why?

Marine Animals

Fish

Fish can breathe underwater because of their gills.

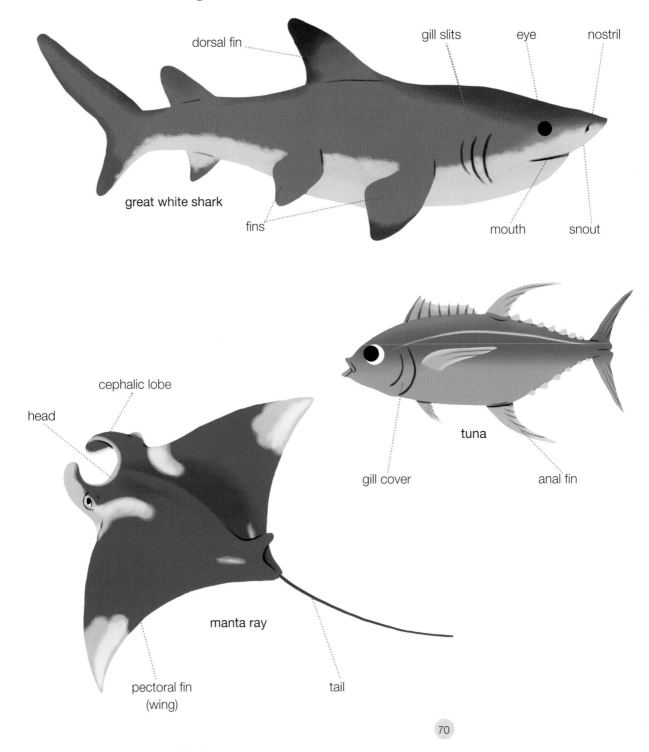

dorsal fin

gill slits

eye

nostril

great white shark

fins

mouth

snout

cephalic lobe

head

tuna

gill cover

anal fin

manta ray

pectoral fin
(wing)

tail

Mammals

Mammals don't breathe underwater. They come up to the surface for air.

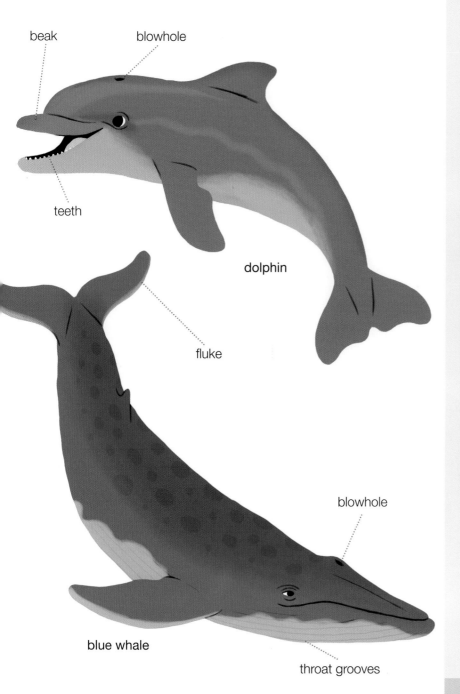

beak

blowhole

teeth

dolphin

fluke

blowhole

blue whale

throat grooves

If you look at the side of a fish, you'll see a slit with "hairs" inside. These are the gills.

After a fish swallows water, the water passes through the gills. The gills hold on to the oxygen in the water and spit out the rest of it.

This way, fish don't need to go to the surface to breathe. That's the biggest difference between a fish and you!

Tropical Ocean Wildlife

In tropical oceans, the water stays warm all year round. Marine animals here tend to be very colorful.

blacktip reef shark

diver

surgeonfish

octopus

green sea turtle

trumpet fish

coral grouper

72

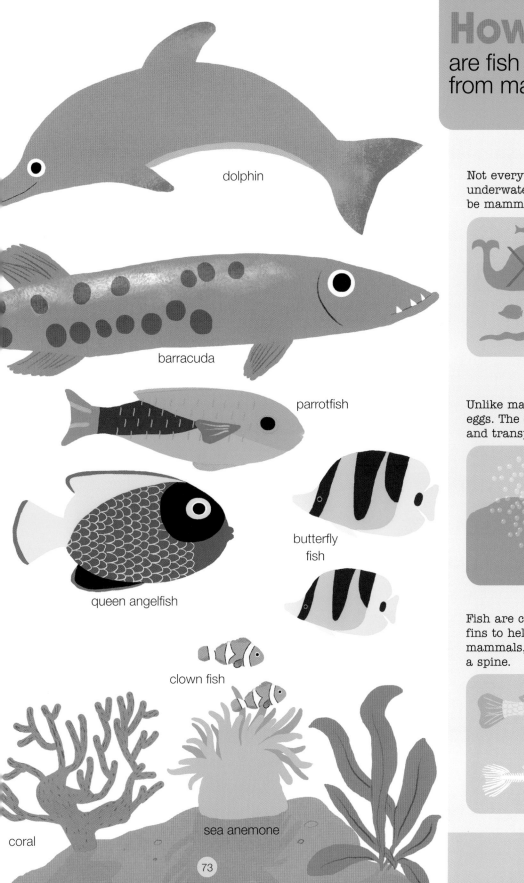

dolphin

barracuda

parrotfish

queen angelfish

butterfly
fish

clown fish

coral

sea anemone

How

are fish different from mammals

?

Not everything that swims underwater is a fish! Some can be mammals.

Unlike mammals, most fish lay eggs. The eggs are often tiny and transparent.

Fish are cold-blooded and have fins to help them move. But like mammals, fish have bones and a spine.

Temperate Ocean Wildlife

In temperate oceans, animals live in water that changes between cold and warm throughout the year.

blue shark

mackerel

ray

sea anemone

turbot

diver

moray eel

seahorse

crab

rock lobster

cod

seal

sardines

tuna

almon

sole

eel

jellyfish

cuttlefish

lobster

a spider crab in
a crab trap

75

How
are mammals
different from fish ?

There are mammals in the ocean. Unlike fish, mammals have lungs and come up to the surface to breathe.

Most mammals carry their babies in their tummies and have teats to feed them milk, even while underwater!

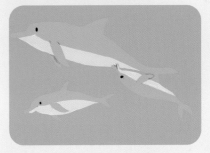

Whales, dolphins, sea lions, and seals are all marine mammals. What land mammals can you name?

Ocean Giants

In the oceans and seas, you can find some of the biggest animals on our planet.

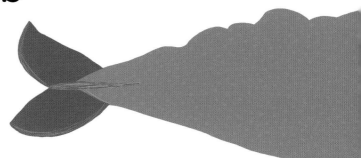

sperm whale

diver

blue whale

orca

giant squid

whale shark

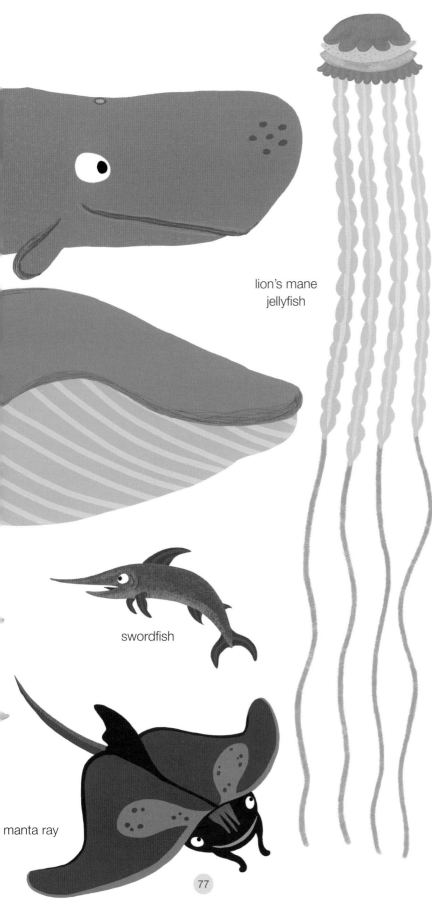

lion's mane
jellyfish

swordfish

manta ray

Which
ocean animals are the most extraordinary?

The blue whale is the biggest and heaviest marine animal. It can weigh the same as at least 20 cars!

The sperm whale is the champion diver! This mammal can spend more than an hour underwater without breathing.

The dolphin can jump really high! And have you ever heard of the flying fish? It jumps out of the water and glides for a moment!

Aquarium

To see marine animals without diving into the water, you can visit an aquarium.

green sea turtle

sawfish

ticket desk

visitor information

touch tank

piranha

sea star

ray

mangrove tree

Florida box turtle

four-eyed fish

dogfish

hammerhead shark

gray reef shark

trainer

tour guide

visitors

nautilus

scorpion fish

surgeonfish

coral reefs exhibit

breeding tanks

veterinarian

injured turtle

Why
are there aquariums
?

An aquarium is a place where you'll see all kinds of fish, mammals, mollusks, algae, crustaceans, corals, and much more!

You'll also see very rare fish. They are well taken care of because so few remain in the world.

Scientists study these creatures and share information about them with the public. What's your favorite marine animal?

Do you recognize these marine animals?

Which of these animals can be found in temperate waters?

Are all these animals fish?

Point to each of these swimmers in order from smallest to biggest. Can you name them?

There are aquariums in lots of big cities. Have you ever visited one?
Which was your favorite animal? Can you describe it in detail?

Oceans and Seas

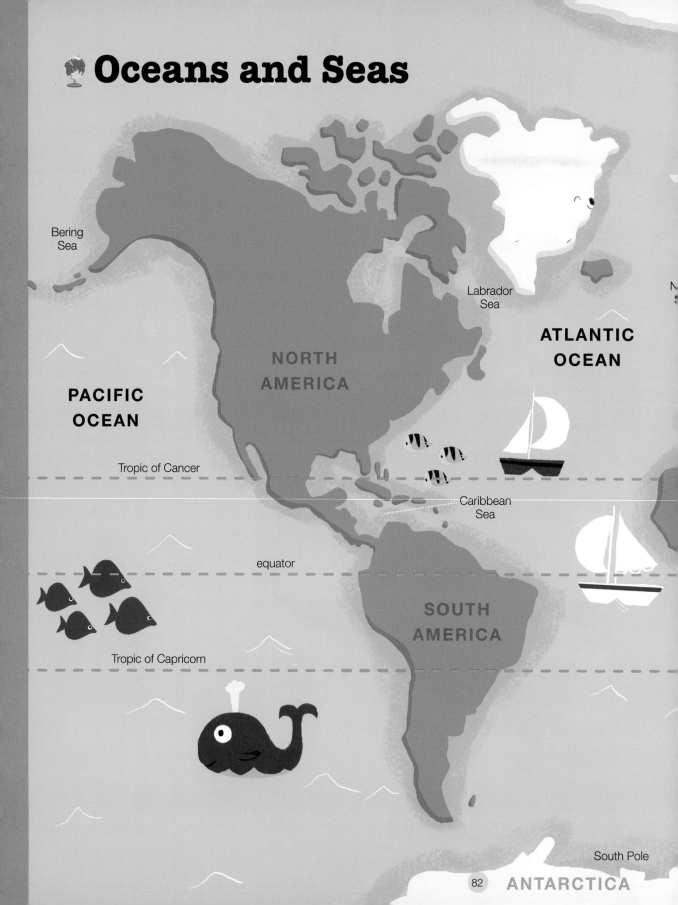

Bering
Sea

Labrador
Sea

ATLANTIC
OCEAN

NORTH
AMERICA

PACIFIC
OCEAN

Tropic of Cancer

Caribbean
Sea

equator

SOUTH
AMERICA

Tropic of Capricorn

South Pole

ANTARCTICA

North Pole

ARCTIC OCEAN

Laptev
Sea

Barents
Sea

Bering
Sea

Sea

Okhotsk
Sea

ASIA

Caspian
Sea

Sea of
Japan

EUROPE

Black
Sea

Mediterranean
Sea

PACIFIC
OCEAN

Arabian
Sea

Red
Sea

South
China
Sea

AFRICA

INDIAN
OCEAN

Coral
Sea

AUSTRALIA

SOUTHERN OCEAN

☁ The Water Cycle

As the Sun warms the water, tiny droplets
go up into the sky: That's called evaporation.
Up there, the droplets gather into clouds.

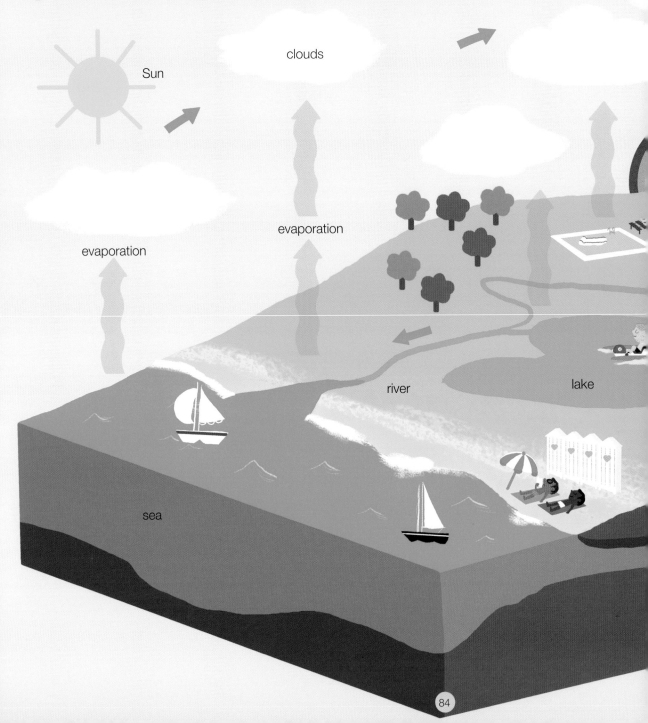

Sun

clouds

evaporation

evaporation

river

lake

sea

clouds

snow

rain

melting
snow

infiltration

infiltration

groundwater

underground river

The Food Chain

All living things are part of the food chain.
That is the order in which they are eaten.
Here's an example.

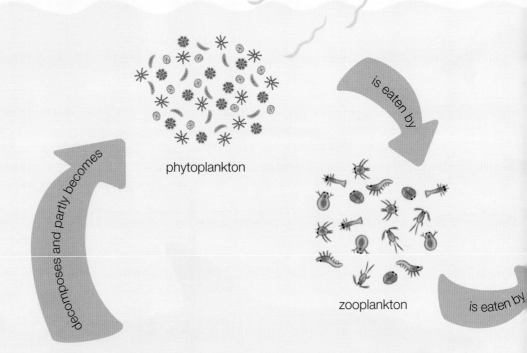

phytoplankton

is eaten by

zooplankton

is eaten by

decomposes and partly becomes

dies

remains of great white shark

herring

is eaten by

dolphin

is eaten by

great white shark

mes

Damaging the Ocean

These actions are harmful to the waters and to marine life:

littering on the beach

throwing waste into the ocean

fishing without thinking about what you'll do with the animals

pulling up plants on the sand dunes

moving rocks around

dumping wastewater into the sea

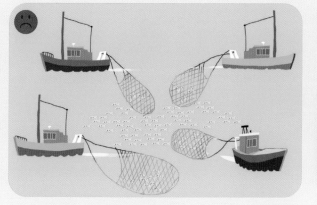

fishing with no limits on how many fish you can catch

cutting corals

causing an oil spill

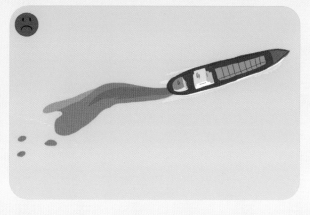

flushing out oil tanks in the open ocean

89

Preserving the Ocean

These actions help take care of the oceans:

participating in a beach cleanup

releasing animals back into the water after catching them

admiring sand dunes

lifting a rock gently

purifying and recycling wastewater

creating marine protected areas

cleaning animals affected by an oil spill

punishing freighters that flush out oil tanks
in the open ocean

Index

A

abalone 32
abyssal plain 10
afraid 51
Africa 83
airboat 59
aircraft carrier 59
airlock 64
algae 79
anal fin 70
anchor 61, 63
angel shark 11
Antarctica 82
aquaculture 30
aquarium 13, 78–79
Arabian Sea 83
Arctic 14
arctic fox 14
Arctic Ocean 14, 83
arm floaties 44, 50, 51
Asia 83
Atlantic Ocean 19, 82
auk 14
Australia 83

B

backpack 53
backstroke 51
ball 48–49, 50
ballast 64, 65
Baltic Sea 83
banana 53
banana tree 13
Barents Sea 83
barracuda 73
bass 28
beach 10, 17, 33, 44, 46–47, 48–49, 88, 90
beach bag 45
beach ball 50
beach camp 47
beach chair 44
beach games 48–49
beach mat 44
beach towel 45
beach umbrella 12, 44, 46, 52
beak 71
Bering Sea 82, 83
bisque 29
Black Sea 83
blacktip reef shark 12, 72
blenny 33
blowhole 71
blue shark 74
blue whale 71, 76
boat 20, 26, 35, 36–37, 38, 50, 58–59, 60–61

boat accident 20
boating 37
boat race 37
bocce ball 48
bodyboarding 36
boom 60
bottle 39, 53
bow 63
breakwater 20, 27
breaststroke 51
breathing underwater 39, 70, 71, 75
breeding tank 79
bridge 61, 63
bubble 39
bucket 48
building a sandcastle 18, 48
buoy 18, 19, 20, 51, 61
burying in the sand 48
butterfly fish 73

C

cabin 46, 60, 62, 65
cake 52
campers 47
canteen 52
cap 44
cargo ship 59
Caribbean Sea 82
Caspian Sea 83
catamaran 37
catch 26
catching shrimp 49
cephalic lobe 70
change of clothes 44
chips 53
clam 32
clamming fork 32
cleanup 90
cliff 14, 16
climbing on rocks 49
cloud 20, 84–85
clown fish 79
coast 16, 35, 60
coastal footpath 17
coast guard boat 59
coastline 16
cockleshell 32
cod 75
collecting seashells 49
competing in a boat race 37
compressed air 39
computer 35
container 52
control room 64
cooler 53
coral 13, 38, 49, 73, 79, 89
coral grouper 72

coral reef 13, 79
Coral Sea 83
cottage 13
cover-up 45
crab 29, 33, 74, 75
crab trap 75
crane 26
crawl stroke 51
crustacean 79
cup 53
current 21
cuttlefish 75

D

damaging the ocean 88–89
danger 21, 65
deep-sea submersible 11
depth 11, 39, 65
depth gauge 39
dining room 63
dip net 33
dive fin 39
dive flag 38
dive light 39
diver 38, 39, 72, 74, 77
diving boot 39
diving hood 39
diving mask 39
dock 26
dogfish 78
dolphin 71, 73, 75, 77, 87
dorsal fin 70
drink 53
drinking from a canteen 52
dry sand 18

E

Earth 14, 19
eating ice cream 52
ebbing tide 19
eel 75
egg 52, 73
engine 64
engine room 62
equator 12, 82
Europe 83
evaporation 30, 84

F

farming 30, 31
fear of water 51
fender 60
ferry 58
fin 70

fish 11, 26–27, 28–29, 30–31, 70–71, 72–73, 75, 78–79
fisherman 26, 28
fishing 12, 13, 26–27, 29–30, 49, 88–89, 90–91
fishing net 12
fishing trawler 17, 26, 27,58
fishing village 12
fish market 28
fishmonger 28, 29
fishmonger's stall 28
fish pâté 29
fish soup 29
fish stick 31
fish tub 26
flag 17, 21, 38, 50, 61
flask 52
flip-flop 45
floating 50, 63
Florida box turtle 78
fluke 71
flying fish 77
food cart 46
food chain 86–87
foredeck 63
four-eyed fish 78
fries 31, 52
Frisbee 48
fruit 53
funnel 62

G

game 48, 63
game room 63
gannet 16
getting a mouthful of water 50
getting around 58
giant squid 11, 76
gill 70, 71
glove 39
goods 58
gorse 17
GPS 35
gravity 19
gray reef shark 79
great white shark 70, 86, 87
green flag 17, 50
green sea turtle 72, 78
groundwater 85
grouper 38, 72
guardrail 34

H

ham 53
hammerhead shark 79
harbor entrance 27

hat 45
head 70
heather 17
hermit crab 33
herring 87
high tide 19
hotel 13
hull 60, 63
husky 14

I

ice 14, 26, 28
iceberg 15
icebreaker 15
ice cream 52, 53
ice sheet 8, 9, 15
Indian Ocean 83
infiltration 85
inflatable raft 50
inflatable vest 51
inlet 12

J

jellyfish 33, 75, 77
Jet Ski 36
jetty 26
jib 61
jumping in the wave 19, 50
junk 59

K

kayak 36
keel 60
kitesurfing 36
knot 61

L

Labrador Sea 82
lagoon 12
lake 84
langoustine 29
Laptev Sea 83
launching a boat 19
lens 34
lifeboat 20, 62
life buoy 60
lifeguard 46, 50
light bulb 34
lighthouse 16, 20, 34, 35, 60
lightning 20
limpet 33
lion's mane jellyfish 77
littering 88
lobster 29, 74, 75
low tide 18, 32

M

mackerel 74
magazine 45
mainsail 60
mangrove tree 78
manta ray 70, 77
marble race 49
mast 60
Mediterranean Sea 19, 83
melon 52
melting snow 85
mess deck 65
mold 48
mollusk 79
Moon 18, 19
mooring bollard 27
mooring buoy 19
moray eel 10, 38, 74
motor 59
motorboat 58
mouth 70
movie theater 62
moving the catch 26
mud 18
musk ox 14
mussel 28, 29, 31, 32, 33

N

napkin 52
nautilus 79
net 12, 27, 33
North America 82
North Pole 15, 83
North Sea 82
nostril 70
nuclear reactor 64

O

ocean floor 10–11, 38
oceanic trench 11
ocean liner 13, 58, 62–63
octopus 72
oilskin raincoat and hat 20
oil spill 89, 91
oil tank 89, 91
Okhotsk Sea 83
Optimist sailing dinghy 37, 58
orca 15, 76
otter shell 32
outrigger canoe 12, 59
overfishing 27, 89
oyster 30
oyster farm 30

P

Pacific Ocean 82, 83
paddle 59
palm tree 13
paper plate 53
parasailing 36
parking 46
parrotfish 12, 38, 73
pearl 30
pebble 17, 18, 49
pectoral fin 70
pedal boat 36, 37
pedestal 34
pelican 12
periscope 65
periwinkle snail 28
phytoplankton 86
picking up food scraps 52
picnic 52–53
picnic basket 52
picnic blanket 52
pine tree 16
piranha 78
pizza 52
planet 8
plankton 13
plastic utensil 52
plate 53
playground 47
playing 46, 48–49, 50–51
polar bear 15
polluting 88, 89
pool 62
port 26, 28, 31, 35
porthole 65
preserving the ocean 90
promenade deck 62
propeller 59, 62, 64
protected areas 91
putting on sunscreen 46

Q

quarterdeck 62
quay 27
queen angelfish 73

R

racing trimaran 58
racket 49
radar 63, 65
radome 63
rain 21, 85
rake 32, 48
raking the sand 32
ray 74, 78
razor clam 32
recycling 53, 91

recycling bin 53
red flag 21
red mullet 28
Red Sea 83
reef 11, 16, 20
reindeer 14
relaxing 52
research station 14
restroom 47
rigid inflatable boat 58
ripple 51
rising tide 19
river 8, 9, 84
riverbank 9
rock 16, 17, 18, 33, 35, 49, 52, 88, 90
rock lobster 74
rowboat 59
rudder 60, 62, 64

S

sail 37, 59, 60
sailboat 16, 37, 58, 59, 60–61
sailing instructor 37
salad 52
salmon 28, 75
salt 30
salt farm 30
salt worker 30
sand 12, 17, 18, 32–33, 46–47, 48–49, 52–53
sandal 44
sandcastle 18, 48, 49
sand dune 46, 88, 90
sandwich 52
sand yacht 47
sardine 75
sausage 53
sawfish 78
scientific research vessel 11
scientist 79
scorpion fish 79
scuba diving 13, 38–39, 77
scuba regulator 39
sea 8, 19, 82, 83, 84
sea anemone 33, 73, 74
sea bream 28
sea-foam 17, 21, 50
seagull 17, 28, 52
seahorse 38, 74
sea ice 14
seal 14, 75
sea lion 75
Sea of Japan 83
seashell 12, 18, 49
sea shuttle 34
sea star 32, 78
sea turtle 12, 72, 78
sea urchin 28, 32
seawall 17
seaweed 17, 18, 31

seaweed farm 31
shade 47
shark 12, 70, 74, 77, 79
shell 32, 33, 49
shellfish 27, 28–29, 30–31, 32–33
shellfish tubs 27
shipwreck 10, 38
shovel 48
shower 46
shrimp 29, 31, 33, 49
shrimp farm 31
sieve 48
signal flare 20
skipper 60
smooth clam 32
snacks 44, 47
snorkeler 12
snorkeling 13, 36, 51
snout 70
snow 85
snowmobile 14
snow petrel 15
sole 75
sonar 65
South America 82
South China Sea 83
Southern Ocean 83
South Pole 15, 82
speedboat 36, 58
sperm whale 10, 76, 77
spider crab 29, 75
sports 36, 38
squid 11, 28, 76
stall 28
stern 62
storm 20
strawberry 53
submarine 11, 64–65
submariner 64
submersible 11
summer 16, 45, 53
Sun 18, 19, 45, 47, 53, 84
sunburn 13, 45
sunglasses 44, 45
sun hat 45
sunscreen 44, 45, 46, 47
sunstroke 47
surfing 37
surgeonfish 72, 79
surging wave 21
sushi 31
swell 20
swimmer 12, 21
swimming 16, 50, 51, 62
swimming area 17
swim ring 50, 51
swimsuit 45
swim trunks 44
swing 47
swordfish 77

T

tail 70
tall ship 59
tank 78, 79
teeth 71
temperate ocean 74
tent 46
tentacle 13
terrace 63
throat groove 71
thunderstorm 20
ticket desk 78
tide 18, 19, 32
tiller 37, 60
tomato 52
tool 32
torpedo 65
touch tank 78
tour guide 79
tower 34
toy boat 50, 59
tracked vehicle 14
trainer 79
trampoline 47
transporting 58
trap 75
trash bin 53
traveling 58
treasure 38
tree 21
trench 11
trimaran 58
tropical ocean 12–13, 72
Tropic of Cancer 82
Tropic of Capricorn 82
trumpet fish 72
T-shirt 44
tugboat 20
tuna 28, 70, 75
turbot 74
turtle 12, 72, 78, 79
tying up a boat 27

U

umbrella 12, 44, 46, 47, 52
underground river 85
unloading the catch 26

V

vegetable 53
vendor 28
veterinarian 79
visitor 79
visitor information 78
volcano 10, 12

W

walking at the water's edge 18
walrus 15
warehouse 26
warty venus 32
water cycle 84–85
watering can 48
water-skiing 36
water sport 36–37
wave 16–17, 19, 20–21, 46, 50-51
weather vane 61
weever 32, 50
weighing the fish 28
weight belt 39
wet sand 18, 33
wet suit 39
whale 71, 75, 76–77
whale shark 76
wharf 34
whelk 32
wind 17, 20–21, 59, 60–61
windsurfing 37
wing 70
winkle 32
winter 15

Y

yacht 58

Z

zooplankton 86